Cambridge Preliminary English Test 6

WITHOUT ANSWERS

Examination papers from University of Cambridge ESOL Examinations

CAMBRIDGE
UNIVERSITY PRESS

CAMBRIDGE UNIVERSITY PRESS
Cambridge, New York, Melbourne, Madrid, Cape Town, Singapore,
São Paulo, Delhi, Dubai, Tokyo

Cambridge University Press
The Edinburgh Building, Cambridge CB2 8RU, UK

www.cambridge.org
Information on this title: www.cambridge.org/9780521123167

First published 2010

Printed in the United Kingdom at the University Press, Cambridge

A catalogue record for this publication is available from the British Library

ISBN 978-0-521-123198   Student's Book with answers
ISBN 978-0-521-123167   Student's Book without answers
ISBN 978-0-521-123211   Audio CD Set
ISBN 978-0-521-123242   Self-study Pack

Contents

A Guide to PET

The PET examination is part of a group of examinations developed by Cambridge ESOL called the Cambridge Main Suite. The Main Suite consists of five examinations which have similar characteristics but are designed for different levels of English language ability. Within the five levels, PET is at Level B1 (Threshold) in the *Council of Europe's Common European Framework of Reference for Languages: Learning, teaching, assessment*. It has also been accredited in the UK as an Entry Level 3 ESOL certificate in the National Qualifications Framework.

Examination	Council of Europe Framework Level	UK National Qualifications Framework Level
CPE Certificate of Proficiency in English	C2	3
CAE Certificate in Advanced English	C1	2
FCE First Certificate in English	B2	1
PET Preliminary English Test	B1	Entry 3
KET Key English Test	A2	Entry 2

PET is a popular exam with candidates who are learning English out of personal interest and for those who are studying for employment reasons. It is also useful preparation for higher level exams, such as FCE (First Certificate in English), CAE (Certificate in Advanced English) and CPE (Certificate of Proficiency in English).

If you can deal with everyday written and spoken communications (e.g. read simple textbooks and articles, write simple personal letters, make notes during a meeting), then this is the exam for you.

Topics

These are the topics used in the PET exam:

Clothes
Daily life
Education
Entertainment and media
Environment
Food and drink
Free time
Health, medicine and
    exercise

Hobbies and leisure
House and home
Language
Natural world
People
Personal feelings, opinions
    and experiences
Personal identification
Places and buildings

Relations with other people
Services
Shopping
Social interaction
Sport
Transport
Travel and holidays
Weather
Work and jobs

PET content: an overview

Paper	Name	Timing	Content	Test focus
Paper 1	Reading/ Writing	1 hour 30 minutes	Reading: Five parts which test a range of reading skills with a variety of texts, ranging from very short notices to longer continuous texts. Writing: Three parts which test a range of writing skills.	Assessment of candidates' ability to understand the meaning of written English at word, phrase, sentence, paragraph and whole text level. Assessment of candidates' ability to produce straightforward written English, ranging from producing variations on simple sentences to pieces of continuous text.
Paper 2	Listening	35 minutes (approx.)	Four parts ranging from short exchanges to longer dialogues and monologues.	Assessment of candidates' ability to understand dialogues and monologues in both informal and neutral settings on a range of everyday topics.
Paper 3	Speaking	10–12 minutes per pair of candidates	Four parts: In Part 1, candidates interact with an examiner; In Parts 2 and 4, they interact with another candidate; In Part 3, they have an extended individual long turn.	Assessment of candidates' ability to express themselves in order to carry out functions at *Threshold* level. To ask and to understand questions and make appropriate responses. To talk freely on matters of personal interest.

Paper 1: Reading and Writing

Paper format
The Reading component contains five parts. The Writing component contains three parts.

Number of questions
Reading has 35 questions; Writing has seven questions.

Sources
Authentic and adapted-authentic real world notices; newspapers and magazines; simplified encyclopaedias; brochures and leaflets; websites.

Answering
Candidates indicate answers by shading lozenges (Reading), or writing answers (Writing) on an answer sheet.

Timing
1 hour 30 minutes.

Marks
Reading: Each of the 35 questions carries one mark. This is weighted so that this comprises 25% of total marks for the whole examination.

Writing: Questions 1–5 carry one mark each. Question 6 is marked out of five; and Question 7/8 is marked out of 15. This gives a total of 25 which represents 25% of total marks for the whole examination.

Preparing for the Reading component

To prepare for the Reading component, you should read a variety of authentic texts, for example, newspapers and magazines, non-fiction books, and other sources of factual material, such as leaflets, brochures and websites. It is also a good idea to practise reading (and writing) short communicative messages, including notes, cards and emails. Remember you won't always need to understand every word in order to be able to do a task in the exam.

Before the examination, think about the time you need to do each part. It is usually approximately 50 minutes on the Reading component and 40 minutes on the Writing component.

Reading			
Part	Task Type and Format	Task Focus	Number of Questions
1	Three-option multiple choice. Five short discrete texts: signs and messages, postcards, notes, emails, labels, etc., plus one example.	Reading real-world notices and other short texts for the main message.	5
2	Matching. Five items in the form of descriptions of people to match to eight short adapted-authentic texts.	Reading multiple texts for specific information and detailed comprehension.	5
3	True/False. Ten items with an adapted-authentic long text.	Processing a factual text. Scanning for specific information while disregarding redundant material.	10
4	Four-option multiple choice. Five items with an adapted-authentic long text.	Reading for detailed comprehension: understanding attitude, opinion and writer purpose. Reading for gist, inference and global meaning.	5
5	Four-option multiple-choice cloze. Ten items, plus an integrated example, with an adapted-authentic text drawn from a variety of sources. The text is of a factual or narrative nature.	Understanding of vocabulary and grammar in a short text, and understanding the lexico-structural patterns in the text.	10

Preparing for the Writing component

Part 1

You have to complete five sentences which will test your grammar. There is an example, showing exactly what the task involves. You should write between one and three words to fill this gap. The second sentence, when complete, must mean the same as the first sentence.

It is essential to spell correctly and no marks will be given if a word is misspelled. You will also lose the mark if you produce an answer of more than three words, even if your writing includes the correct answer.

Part 2

You have to produce a short communicative message of between 35 and 45 words in length. You are told who you are writing to and why, and you must include three content points. These are clearly laid out with bullet points in the question. To gain top marks, all three points must be in your answer, so it is important to read the question carefully and plan what you will include. Marks will not be deducted for minor errors.

Before the exam, you need to practise writing answers of the correct length. Answers that are too short or too long will probably lose marks.

The General Mark Scheme below is used with a Task-specific Mark Scheme (see pages 104, 117, 129 and 141).

General Mark Scheme for Writing Part 2

Mark	Criteria
5	All content elements covered appropriately. Message clearly communicated to reader.
4	All content elements adequately dealt with. Message communicated successfully, on the whole.
3	All content elements attempted. Message requires some effort by the reader. or One content element omitted but others clearly communicated.
2	Two content elements omitted, or unsuccessfully dealt with. Message only partly communicated to reader. or Script may be slightly short (20–25 words).
1	Little relevant content and/or message requires excessive effort by the reader, or short (10–19 words).
0	Totally irrelevant or totally incomprehensible or too short (under 10 words).

Part 3

You have a choice of task: either a story or an informal letter. You need to write about 100 words. Answers below 80 words will receive fewer marks. Answers longer than 100 words may receive fewer marks.

Make sure you practise enough before the exam. Reading simplified readers in English will give you ideas for story writing. Also writing to a penfriend or e-pal will give you useful practice.

Mark Scheme for Writing Part 3

Band 5 – the candidate's writing fully achieves the desired effect on the target reader. The use of language will be confident and ambitious for the level, including a wide range of structures and vocabulary within the task set. Coherence, within the constraints of the level, will be achieved by the use of simple linking devices, and the response will be well organised. Errors which do occur will be minor and non-impeding, perhaps due to ambitious attempts at more complex language. Overall, no effort will be required of the reader.

Band 4 – the candidate's writing will achieve the desired effect on the target reader. The use of language will be fairly ambitious for the level, including a range of structures and vocabulary within the task set. There will be some linking of sentences and evidence of organisation. Some errors will occur, although these will be generally non-impeding. Overall, only a little effort will be required of the reader.

Band 3 – the candidate's writing may struggle at times to achieve the desired effect on the target reader. The use of language, including the range of structure and vocabulary, will be unambitious, or, if ambitious, it will be flawed. There will be some attempt at organisation but the linking of sentences will not always be maintained. A number of errors may be present, although these will be mostly non-impeding. Overall, some effort will be required of the reader.

Band 2 – the candidate's writing struggles to achieve the desired effect on the target reader. The use of language, including the range of structure and vocabulary, will tend to be simplistic, limited, or repetitive. The response may be incoherent, and include erratic use of punctuation. There will be numerous errors which will sometimes impede communication. Overall, considerable effort will be required of the reader.

Band 1 – the candidate's writing has a negative effect on the target reader. The use of language will be severely restricted, and there will be no evidence of a range of structures and vocabulary. The response will be seriously incoherent, and may include an absence of punctuation. Language will be very poorly controlled and the response will be difficult to understand. Overall, excessive effort will be required of the reader.

Band 0 – there may be too little language for assessment, or the response may be totally illegible; the content may be impossible to understand, or completely irrelevant to the task.

Writing			
Part	**Task Type and Format**	**Task Focus**	**Number of Questions**
1	Sentence transformations. Five items, plus an integrated example, that are theme-related. Candidates are given sentences and then asked to complete similar sentences using a different structural pattern so that the sentence still has the same meaning.	Control and understanding of Threshold/PET grammatical structures. Rephrasing and reformulating information.	5
2	Short communicative message. Candidates are prompted to write a short message in the form of a postcard, note, email, etc. The prompt takes the form of a rubric to respond to.	A short piece of writing of 35–45 words focusing on communication of specific messages.	1
3	A longer piece of continuous writing. There is a choice of two questions, an informal letter or a story. Candidates are primarily assessed on their ability to use and control a range of Threshold-level language. Coherent organisation, spelling and punctuation are also assessed.	Writing about 100 words focusing on control and range of language.	1

Paper 2: Listening

Paper format
This paper contains four parts.

Number of questions
25

Text types
All texts are based on authentic situations.

Answering
Candidates indicate answers either by shading lozenges (Parts 1, 2 and 4) or writing answers (Part 3) on an answer sheet. Candidates record their answers on the question paper as they listen. They are then given six minutes at the end of the test to copy these on to the answer sheet.

Recording information
Each text is heard twice. Recordings will contain a variety of accents corresponding to standard variants of native speaker accents.

Timing
About 35 minutes, including six minutes to transfer answers.

Marks
Each question carries one mark. This gives a total of 25 marks, which represents 25% of total marks for the whole examination.

Part	Task Type and Format	Task Focus	Number of questions
1	Multiple choice (discrete). Short neutral or informal monologues or dialogues. Seven discrete three-option multiple-choice items with visuals, plus one example.	Listening to identify key information from short exchanges.	7
2	Multiple choice. Longer monologue or interview (with one main speaker). Six three-option multiple-choice items.	Listening to identify specific information and detailed meaning.	6
3	Gap-fill. Longer monologue. Six gaps to fill in. Candidates need to write one or more words in each space.	Listening to identify, understand and interpret information.	6
4	True/False. Longer informal dialogue. Candidates need to decide whether six statements are correct or incorrect.	Listening for detailed meaning, and to identify the attitudes and opinions of the speakers.	6

Preparing for the Listening paper

You will hear the instructions for each task on the recording, and see them on the exam paper.
In Part 1, there is also an example text and task to show you how to record your answers.
In Parts 2, 3 and 4, the instructions are followed by a pause; you should read the questions in that part then. This will help you prepare for the listening.

The best preparation for the listening paper is to listen to authentic spoken English at this level. Having discussions provides a good authentic source of listening practice, as does listening to the teacher. You can also listen to texts to give you practice in understanding different voices and styles of delivery.

Paper 3: Speaking

Paper format

The standard format is two candidates and two examiners. One of the examiners acts as an interlocutor and the other as an assessor. The interlocutor directs the test, while the assessor takes no part in the interaction.

Timing

10–12 minutes per pair of candidates.

Marks

Candidates are assessed on their performance throughout the test. There are a total of 25 marks in Paper 3, making 25% of the total score for the whole examination.

Part	Task Type and Format	Task Focus	Timing
1	Each candidate interacts with the interlocutor. The interlocutor asks the candidates questions in turn, using standardised questions.	Giving information of a factual, personal kind. The candidates respond to questions about present circumstances, past experiences and future plans.	2–3 minutes
2	Simulated situation. Candidates interact with each other. Visual stimulus is given to the candidates to aid the discussion task. The interlocutor sets up the activity using a standardised rubric.	Using functional language to make and respond to suggestions, discuss alternatives, make recommendations and negotiate agreement.	2–3 minutes
3	Extended turn. A colour photograph is given to each candidate in turn and they are asked to talk about it for up to a minute. Both photographs relate to the same topic.	Describing photographs and managing discourse, using appropriate vocabulary, in a longer turn.	3 minutes
4	General conversation. Candidates interact with each other. The topic of the conversation develops the theme established in Part 3. The interlocutor sets up the activity using a standardised rubric.	The candidates talk together about their opinions, likes/dislikes, preferences, experiences, habits, etc.	3 minutes

Assessment

Throughout the test, you are assessed on your language skills, not your personality, intelligence or knowledge of the world. You must, however, be prepared to develop the conversation, where appropriate, and respond to the tasks set. Prepared speeches are not acceptable.

You are assessed on your own individual performance and not in relation to each other. Both examiners assess you. The interlocutor awards a mark for global achievement; the assessor awards marks for: Grammar and Vocabulary, Discourse Management, Pronunciation and Interactive Communication.

Grammar and Vocabulary
This refers to the accurate use of grammatical forms and appropriate use of vocabulary. It also includes the range of vocabulary. Performance is viewed in terms of the overall effectiveness of the language used in dealing with the tasks.

Discourse Management
This refers to the coherence, extent and relevance of each individual's contribution. On this scale, the ability to maintain a coherent flow of language is assessed, either within a single utterance or over a string of utterances. Also assessed here is how relevant the contributions are to what has gone before.

Pronunciation
This refers to the candidate's ability to produce comprehensible utterances to fulfil the task requirements. This includes stress, intonation, and individual sounds. Examiners put themselves in the position of the non-language specialist and assess the overall impact of the pronunciation and the degree of effort required to understand the candidate. Different varieties of English, e.g. British, North American, Australian, etc., are acceptable, provided they are used consistently throughout the test.

Interactive Communication
This scale refers to the candidate's ability to use language to achieve meaningful communication. This includes initiating and responding without undue hesitation, the ability to use interactive strategies to maintain or repair communication, and sensitivity to the norms of turn-taking.

Further information

More information about PET or any other Cambridge ESOL examination can be obtained from Cambridge ESOL at the address below or from the website at www.CambridgeESOL.org

University of Cambridge ESOL Examinations
1 Hills Road
Cambridge CB1 2EU
United Kingdom

Telephone +44 1223 553355
Fax: +44 1223 460278
email: ESOLHelpdesk@Cambridgeassessment.org.uk

Test 1

PAPER 1   READING AND WRITING TEST   (1 hour 30 minutes)

READING

Part 1

Questions 1–5

Look at the text in each question.
What does it say?
Mark the correct letter **A**, **B** or **C** on your answer sheet.

Example:

0

A Buy three films for the price of two.

B Get a free film with every one you buy.

C Films bought here are printed free.

Answer:

1

Who should Lisa contact if she wants to go to the concert?

A Yvonne

B Marie

C Sally

2

Parking Form

Complete and place in lower left-hand corner of windscreen

Car registration ....

Date ....

A Register your car here by filling in this form.

B Put this form in your car windscreen after filling it in.

C Place the completed form at the top of your car windscreen.

3

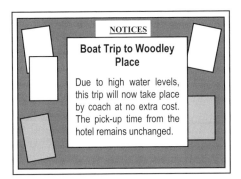

NOTICES

Boat Trip to Woodley Place

Due to high water levels, this trip will now take place by coach at no extra cost. The pick-up time from the hotel remains unchanged.

What has changed about the trip to Woodley Place?

A the transport

B the price

C the departure time

4

Mum,
Could you pick up my skirt from the dry cleaner's when you collect your jacket? I'll pay you back this evening.
Thanks.
Sonja

What will Sonja's mother do?

A receive money for the dry cleaning from Sonja tonight

B fetch Sonja's jacket from the dry cleaner's for her

C deliver her own clothes to the dry cleaner's

5

Allow at least two hours for your visit to the castle

A Each tour of the castle lasts less than two hours.

B Two hours is the minimum time recommended for a visit to the castle.

C Visitors are only allowed to spend two hours inside the castle.

Part 2

Questions 6–10

The people below live in London and are all interested in keeping fit.
On the opposite page there are descriptions of eight websites for people wanting to keep fit.
Decide which website would be the most suitable for the following people.
For questions **6–10**, mark the correct letter (**A–H**) on your answer sheet.

---

6  Klara has recently moved to London and enjoys serious running. She is looking for a club where she can take part in competitions.

7  Sami wants to find some ideas for keeping fit at home and communicate online with other people doing the same thing. He doesn't want to have to pay for using the website.

8  Kumiko is a member of a local gym where she goes at least twice a week. She does not get much time to shop, so wants to buy gym clothes and shoes online.

9  Peter loves the outdoors and cycles to different places each weekend to keep fit. He wants a website which will give him suggestions for a range of suitable destinations.

10  Stefano is a student and is looking for a gym where he can keep fit. He wants to pay each time he visits the gym rather than paying a fee to become a member.

FIND THE PERFECT WAY TO KEEP FIT WITH THESE WEBSITES

A www.activelife.co.uk This site is perfect for those who like to combine living a healthy lifestyle with enjoying the countryside. Type in the name of the town and you get a list of locations that offer routes for cycling or exploring the area on foot. There is also information on cycling competitions in Britain.

B www.fitinfo.com This online shop offers books, magazines, DVDs and software connected to keeping fit. You simply type in the aspect of keeping fit that you are interested in, such as 'keeping fit outdoors', and a super selection is displayed.

C www.fitnet.co.uk Steve Amos started this site for busy people wanting to keep fit. Fill in a questionnaire and Steve will create a fitness programme for you. Although Steve's fee is high, you can email him for advice whenever you want. In addition, Steve has designed a range of fitness clothes and footwear, which anyone can order (48-hour delivery).

D www.NAG.co.uk The National Athletics Group is a site for people interested in athletics. It allows you to find out where your nearest athletics club is and provides information about races and other athletics events around the country. There is a popular chatroom where athletes exchange suggestions and ideas.

E www.swavedon.com Swavedon is a national park with a lake, which offers many different ways of keeping fit in the great outdoors. There are three cycle routes, a jogging track around the lake and several woodland walks.

F www.fitnessonline.co.uk This is a free government website that encourages people to keep fit. It gives diet advice, and allows you to work through a fitness programme without leaving your house. It also offers advice on gym equipment to buy and has a chatroom, where you can compare experiences with others.

G www.fitnessclub.co.uk This website tells you all you need to know about this chain of gyms, including where your nearest Fitnessclub gym is, how you can become a member and how much the yearly fee is. Advice is given on everything from using a running machine to buying the right equipment. Each gym has a swimming pool and a shop selling gymwear.

H www.sportsarena.co.uk This website tells you how you can keep fit at this group of London sports centres. You don't have to be a member – these centres operate a pay-as-you-go system. They all have a pool, squash courts, gym and outdoor tennis courts. The website includes details of locations, opening times and prices.

Part 3

Questions 11–20

Look at the sentences below about a book club.
Read the text on the opposite page to decide if each sentence is correct or incorrect.
If it is correct, mark **A** on your answer sheet.
If it is not correct, mark **B** on your answer sheet.

---

11   By ordering a book, you qualify to become a member of the International Book Club.

12   Every new member can request a watch from the book club.

13   You can buy a DVD more cheaply when you join.

14   All club books cost half the publisher's price.

15   Each club magazine gives you a choice of over 1,000 books.

16   You get a different choice of books if you order from the website.

17   One special book is recommended every month.

18   You may receive a book that the club has chosen for you.

19   You must pay the postage when sending your application to join the club.

20   You should pay as soon as you receive your books.

International Book Club

Have you ever thought of joining a book club and buying new books through the post? Here at the International Book Club, we already have many members buying books from us by mail.

To join:
You just need to send us your first order from our book list.

Immediate benefits:

- As a special offer, you may choose any reduced-price books from our new members' book list, to the value of £6 in total (plus postage and packing). By doing this, you will save pounds on the publishers' prices.
- Tick the box on your form to order a free watch.
- If you reply within seven days, we will send you another free gift carefully chosen from our book list by our staff.
- Order a DVD from the many on offer in our list, at half the recommended retail price.

When you've joined:
As a member, you'll enjoy savings of between 30% and 50% off the publisher's price on every book you buy, and what's more, they'll come straight to your door. Your free club magazine arrives once a month, to keep you up to date with the latest best-sellers. This means that every year we offer over 1,000 books to choose from. On the Internet, you can find all our titles for the year on our exclusive members' website.

Being a member:
All we are asking you to do while you are a member is to choose four books during your first year. After that, you can decide on the number of books you wish to take.

In each of our monthly club magazines, our experienced staff choose a Club Choice book – a work of fiction or a reference title which they feel is particularly worth buying, and which is offered at an extra-special price. However, if you do not want this book, just say so in the space provided on the form. We will always send the book if we do not receive this.

So, return your application form today, but hurry – it's not every day we can make you an offer like this. To apply to become a member, all you need to do is simply fill in the enclosed form and return it in the postage-paid envelope supplied.

Before you know it, your books will be with you. Please don't send any money now, as we will send you your bill with the books. And remember, you have up to a fortnight to decide if you wish to keep the books you have ordered. You should then either return the books or send your payment.

Part 4

Questions 21–25

Read the text and questions below.
For each question, mark the correct letter **A**, **B**, **C** or **D** on your answer sheet.

Rock Band

Two years ago, our 14-year-old son, Ben, asked us for a set of drums for his birthday. At first, we were very much against the idea because of the noise. 'It's better than watching television or playing computer games in my free time,' Ben argued, 'and it'll keep me out of trouble.' In the end we gave in. 'All right,' we said, 'but you must consider the rest of the family and the neighbours when you play.'

That was just the beginning. Because drums are not the easiest instruments to transport, the other members of Ben's band started appearing at our home with their guitars and other electrical equipment. And so, for several hours a week, the house shakes to the noise of their instruments and their teenage singing.

At least Ben's hobby has been good for our health: whenever the band start practising, my husband and I go out for a long walk. And I must admit that, although their music may sound a little strange, they are a friendly and polite group of young men. I cannot judge their musical skill – after all I didn't expect my parents' generation to like the same music as I did when I was a teenager – but they do play regularly in local clubs for young people.

Our main worry is that they won't spend enough time on their school work because of their musical activities, though this hasn't happened yet. I am always stressing to Ben how important his studies are. But one thing is certain – Ben was right: it has kept him out of trouble and he is never bored.

21   What is the writer trying to do in this text?

   A   complain about her son's friends
   B   give advice to teenagers
   C   describe her son's hobby
   D   compare herself with her parents

22   Why did the writer give Ben the present he wanted?

   A   She wanted to reward him for working hard.
   B   He already had too many computer games.
   C   She knew he would use it sensibly.
   D   He persuaded her it would be a good idea.

23 Why do the band always practise at Ben's house?

    A   It is difficult for Ben to move his drums.

    B   The neighbours don't mind the noise.

    C   Ben's parents enjoy listening to them.

    D   They can leave their equipment there.

24 What does the writer say about the band members?

    A   Their influence on her son worries her.

    B   Their taste in music is different from hers.

    C   They play their instruments well.

    D   They avoid any contact with her.

25 What might the writer say to her son?

A
> Your teacher has just phoned. He wants to know why you weren't at school today.

B
> When are you playing at the club next? Dad and I would love to come along again.

C
> If you don't know what to do with yourself, there's a good programme on the television in a few minutes.

D
> Are you sure you've finished your homework? It's more important than band practice.

19

Part 5

Questions 26–35

Read the text below and choose the correct word for each space.
For each question, mark the correct letter **A**, **B**, **C** or **D** on your answer sheet.

Example:

| 0 | **A** most | **B** more | **C** best | **D** better |

Answer:

0	A B C D
	▬ ▭ ▭ ▭

Tom Cruise

Tom Cruise is one of the **(0)** .... successful actors in cinema history. However, life hasn't always been that easy for him. As a young boy, Tom was shy and had **(26)** .... in finding friends, although he really enjoyed **(27)** .... part in school plays.

(28) .... he had finished High School, Tom went to New York to look for work. He found employment as a porter, and at the same time he **(29)** .... drama classes. In 1980, the film director Franco Zeffirelli **(30)** .... Tom his first part in a film. Ten years later, he had become **(31)** .... successful that he was one of the highest-paid actors in Hollywood, **(32)** .... millions of dollars for **(33)** .... film.

Today, Tom **(34)** .... appears in films and is as **(35)** .... as ever with his thousands of fans from all around the world.

26	**A** worry	**B** problem	**C** fear	**D** difficulty
27	**A** making	**B** holding	**C** taking	**D** finding
28	**A** While	**B** During	**C** After	**D** Until
29	**A** prepared	**B** waited	**C** attended	**D** happened
30	**A** suggested	**B** offered	**C** tried	**D** advised
31	**A** so	**B** such	**C** too	**D** very
32	**A** paying	**B** earning	**C** winning	**D** reaching
33	**A** another	**B** all	**C** each	**D** some
34	**A** yet	**B** ever	**C** already	**D** still
35	**A** popular	**B** favourite	**C** preferred	**D** approved

WRITING

Part 1

Questions 1–5

Here are some sentences about learning Italian.
For each question, complete the second sentence so that it means the same as the first.
Use no more than three words.
Write only the missing words on your answer sheet.
You may use this page for any rough work.

Example:

0   Daniel started Italian classes six months ago.

   Daniel's had Italian classes .... **six months**.

Answer: | **0** | *for* |

---

1   After seeing an advertisement for Italian lessons, Daniel decided to go.

   Daniel .... **an advertisement for Italian lessons and then decided to go**.

2   There are fifteen other students in his Italian class.

   His Italian class .... **fifteen other students in it**.

3   Daniel thinks that speaking Italian is easier than writing it.

   Daniel doesn't think that speaking is .... **as writing Italian**.

4   Daniel's teacher is Italian and her name's Chiara Paolozzi.

   Daniel's teacher is Italian and she's .... **Chiara Paolozzi**.

5   The students are given two hours of homework each week.

   Each week Chiara .... **the students two hours of homework**.

Part 2

Question 6

You have spent the weekend staying with some English friends.

Write a card to them. In your card, you should

- thank your friends for the weekend
- say what you enjoyed most about the weekend
- invite them to stay with you.

Write **35–45 words** on your answer sheet.

Part 3

Write an answer to **one** of the questions (**7** or **8**) in this part.
Write your answer in about **100 words** on your answer sheet.
Mark the question number in the box at the top of your answer sheet.

Question 7

- This is part of a letter you receive from an English friend.

> I've just seen a brilliant programme about dolphins on television. Which programmes have you enjoyed recently? How much television do you watch?

- Now write a letter, answering your penfriend's questions.
- Write your **letter** on your answer sheet.

Question 8

- Your English teacher has asked you to write a story.
- This is the title for your story:

Walking in the rain

- Write your **story** on your answer sheet.

PAPER 2   LISTENING TEST   approx 35 minutes
(including 6 minutes transfer time)

Part 1

Questions 1–7

There are seven questions in this part.
For each question there are three pictures and a short recording.
Choose the correct picture and put a tick (✓) in the box below it.

Example: Where is the girl's hat?

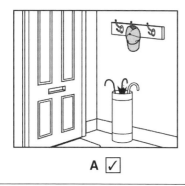

A ✓

B ☐

C ☐

---

1   Where will the friends meet?

A ☐

B ☐

C ☐

2   What has the girl forgotten to bring?

A ☐

B ☐

C ☐

3 Which TV programme is on at 9 o'clock tonight?

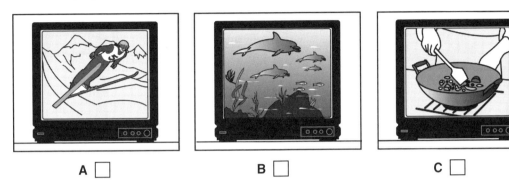

A ☐   B ☐   C ☐

4 How will the man book tickets for the show?

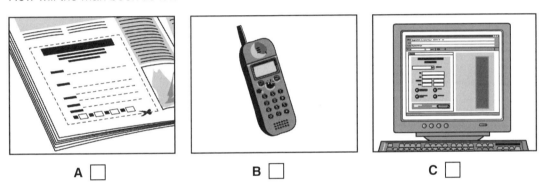

A ☐   B ☐   C ☐

5 What will the man do this winter?

A ☐   B ☐   C ☐

6   How does the man want the woman to help him?

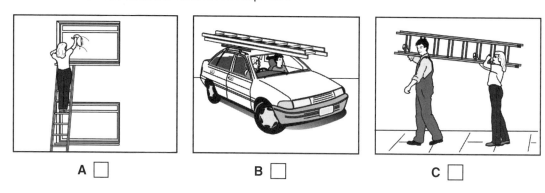

A ☐   B ☐   C ☐

7   Which house did the woman stay in?

A ☐   B ☐   C ☐

Part 2

Questions 8–13

You will hear a news reporter called Angela Bond, talking on the radio about her job.
For each question, put a tick (✓) in the correct box.

---

8   Where is Angela working at the moment?   **A** ☐ Britain

B ☐ the USA

C ☐ Asia

9   Angela likes her job because she   **A** ☐ loves being in dangerous situations.

B ☐ never knows where she'll go next.

C ☐ enjoys watching important events happen.

10   What did Angela bring home from Hong Kong?   **A** ☐ pictures

B ☐ carpets

C ☐ furniture

11   What time does Angela's working day begin?   **A** ☐ 8.30 am

B ☐ 6.30 pm

C ☐ 10.00 am

12   Where did Angela meet her boyfriend?

A ☐ at her sister's house

B ☐ at university

C ☐ in Hong Kong

13   What does Angela do to relax?

A ☐ She cooks a meal.

B ☐ She goes sailing.

C ☐ She goes shopping.

Part 3

Questions 14–19

You will hear a radio programme about some historic places to visit.
For each question, fill in the missing information in the numbered space.

HISTORIC PLACES TO VISIT

Black Rock Caves

- Over 2 million years old
- For half a million years, people and animals, especially **(14)** .... , lived here
- Special evening tours during the month of **(15)** ....

Salter House

- Built in the year **(16)** ....
- Made famous by the television series called *Aunt Dorothy*
- All visitors want to see Dorothy's **(17)** ....

The Old Port

- Have a ride on an old tram to the **(18)** .... village
- In the factory, find out how people used to make **(19)** ....

Part 4

Questions 20–25

Look at the six sentences for this part.
You will hear a conversation between a boy, Marcus, and a girl, Catherine, about their homework.
Decide if each sentence is correct or incorrect.
If it is correct, put a tick (✓) in the box under **A** for **YES**. If it is not correct, put a tick (✓) in the box under **B** for **NO**.

		A YES	B NO
20	Catherine finds it hard to understand why Marcus has so much homework.	☐	☐
21	Marcus agrees that he could change his weekend activities.	☐	☐
22	Catherine thinks visiting the museum was a good experience for Marcus.	☐	☐
23	Catherine offers to show Marcus the maths homework she has already done.	☐	☐
24	Marcus worries that his teacher might be angry if Catherine helps him.	☐	☐
25	After talking to Catherine, Marcus feels more confident about his homework.	☐	☐

About the Speaking test

The Speaking test lasts about 10 to 12 minutes. You take the test with another candidate. There are two examiners in the room. One examiner talks to you and the other examiner listens to you. Both the examiners give you marks.

Part 1

The examiners introduce themselves and then one examiner asks you and your partner to say your names and spell them. This examiner then asks you questions about yourself, your daily life, interests, etc.

Part 2

The examiner asks you to talk about something together and gives you a drawing to help you.

Part 3

You each have a chance to talk by yourselves. The examiner gives you a colour photograph to look at and asks you to talk about it. When you have finished talking, the examiner gives your partner a different photograph to look at and to talk about.

Part 4

The examiner asks you and your partner to say more about the subject of the photographs in Part 3. You may be asked to give your opinion or to talk about something that has happened to you.

Test 2

PAPER 1   READING AND WRITING TEST   (1 hour 30 minutes)

READING

Part 1

Questions 1–5

Look at the text in each question.
What does it say?
Mark the correct letter **A**, **B** or **C** on your answer sheet.

Example:

0

A Do not leave your bicycle touching the window.

B Broken glass may damage your bicycle tyres.

C Your bicycle may not be safe here.

Answer:

1

WATCH REPAIRS

Warning to Customers

All uncollected items will be sold after twelve months.

A This shop will sell customers' watches within twelve months.

B This shop will keep customers' watches for up to twelve months.

C This shop will look after customers' watches for more than twelve months.

2

Philippe,

Couldn't wait any longer, didn't want to miss the start of the match! Problem at work? Here's your ticket – see you at the stadium.

Stefano

A Philippe and Stefano missed each other at the stadium.

B Stefano had to leave without Philippe to get to work.

C Stefano has given up waiting for Philippe to arrive.

3

PARENTS:

Complete and return your child's form for next month's school trip by Friday

A Parents must return forms this week if their child is going on Friday's trip.

B Parents cannot go on next month's trip unless they return their forms by Friday.

C The last day for returning completed forms for the trip is Friday.

4

From:	Gabi
To:	Jo

I'll be in town on business on Wednesday, so could we meet for dinner then, instead of on Thursday as usual?

Gabi wants Jo to

A change an arrangement.

B cancel a regular event.

C come to a business meeting.

5

A It is not possible to use the lift above the ground floor today.

B The lift will not be going to the basement today.

C The stairs between the basement and the ground floor are closed today.

Part 2

Questions 6–10

The people below all want to visit a park.
On the opposite page there are descriptions of eight parks.
Decide which park would be the most suitable for the following people.
For questions **6–10**, mark the correct letter (**A–H**) on your answer sheet.

6  Isabel works in the city centre and likes painting and drawing in her free time. She wants to practise her hobby in a small, quiet park near her office.

7  Mr Martin wants to take his eight-year-old pupils to a park anywhere within the city, with lots of organised activities which allow the children to read about local wildlife they may see.

8  Kumiko and Atsuko would like to visit a park which they can get to by boat. They want to buy lunch there and then enjoy a short walk accompanied by an expert leader.

9  Hans and Birgit Kaufmann and their family want to visit a park which is historically important. Their teenage children would like to try a water sport.

10  Melanie and Stefan are students who need to visit a busy park for a college project. They want to draw people taking part in team sports and watching entertainment.

PARKS IN AND AROUND THE CITY

A   Hadley Park

This park is in the peaceful village of Cranford, 20 km outside the city. The park has large green spaces for football and there is also an area of woodland, a boating lake, fish ponds and a variety of local wildlife. The public car park is free.

B   Highdown Park

The largest and most popular open space in the city, Highdown has many paths for keen walkers, as well as horse-riding and golf. The much-visited 19th-century glasshouses contain an interesting exhibition about birds from around the world.

C   Brock Park

A beautiful park on the edge of the city, Brock Park attracts huge crowds. The open-air theatre has a programme of plays suitable for school groups. There is a well-used basketball court and baseball field, a children's playground and a café. Climb Harry's Hill to admire the beautiful fields and forests beyond the city.

D   Lilac Park and House

This busy city-centre park has a long history dating back to the 1700s, when it belonged to the writer Thomas Crane. The house is open to the public and a guided visit can also include a walk around the famous rose gardens, finishing at the popular Butterfly Café.

E   Boscawen Park

This small and peaceful park offers guided tours, given by the knowledgeable Environment Officers, and evening visitors to the park may be lucky enough to see rare frogs and bats. It is situated on the River Elton and can be reached in about 30 minutes from the city centre by river taxi. There is a snack bar and gift shop.

F   East Bank Park

This is a tiny, little-known park in the heart of the city, with gardens filled with sculptures, trees and flowers. It makes a perfect resting place, popular with local artists, and is within minutes of the theatre and entertainment district.

G   Victoria Park

This quiet park, on the edge of the city and easy to visit by public transport, has boats for hire on the lake, a skateboard park, basketball and tennis courts and a picnic area. Often seen in postcard views of the city, Victoria Park contains one of the oldest windmills in the country – the museum should not be missed.

H   Elmwood Park

At Elmwood Park, there are walks on well-made paths and cycle rides for all abilities. Elmwood is just inside the city limit and has an area of quiet woodland, which is home to deer and other animals. The visitor centre, numerous display boards and a fun quiz make this a positive learning experience for all ages.

Part 3

Questions 11–20

Look at the sentences below about the Iditarod Trail in Alaska.
Read the text on the opposite page to decide if each sentence is correct or incorrect.
If it is correct, mark **A** on your answer sheet.
If it is not correct, mark **B** on your answer sheet.

---

11 The population of Alaska remained the same throughout the 1880s.

12 For a short time, more people lived in Iditarod than in any other city in Alaska.

13 After 1910, it became possible to deliver letters in winter as well as summer.

14 When travelling on the Iditarod Trail, drivers had to take food for the dogs with them.

15 In the 1920s, aeroplanes were used more often than boats and dogs.

16 Doctors in Nome had a good supply of medicine to cure diphtheria.

17 The pilot Carl Eielson refused to fly his plane because of the cold weather.

18 Leonhard Seppala's dog was able to lead him safely to his destination.

19 Balto fell into some icy water but managed to save himself.

20 The Iditarod race takes a different route every year.

THE HISTORY OF THE IDITAROD – THE LAST GREAT RACE ON EARTH

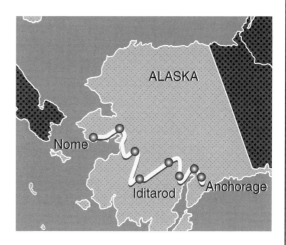

In the 1880s, gold was discovered in what is now the most northern state of the USA, Alaska. Many people came to the area hoping to get rich. New towns were built and grew quickly. One such town was called Iditarod, which means 'far, distant place'. This town grew so quickly during 1909 that it briefly became the largest city in Alaska. In the summer months, essential supplies could be delivered to these towns by boat, but in the winter the rivers and the ocean froze and there was no way to get to them. So, in 1910, a winter track was built which would be used by teams of dogs pulling sleds. They would take mail, food and clothes to the gold miners.

The track became known as the Iditarod Trail. It took a team of dogs about three weeks to travel across Alaska. They stopped at 'roadhouses' where the drivers could get a warm bed for the night and something to eat for both themselves and their dogs. The trail was used every winter until the 1920s when aeroplanes replaced steam boats and dog teams as the main form of transport.

However, the dogs had one last taste of fame in 1925, when a disease called diphtheria hit the city of Nome. The disease could be cured, but, unfortunately, the closest medicine that could be found was in Anchorage, right on the other side of Alaska. Aeroplanes were still quite new, so no-one knew if they could fly in such cold weather. Also, Carl Eielson, the only pilot considered skilled enough to manage the flight, was away on a trip at the time. It was therefore agreed that the medicine would be transported using teams of dogs instead.

The trip covered over 1,000 kilometres, most of it along the Iditarod Trail. It took twenty teams just six days to complete the journey. Leonhard Seppala, a Norwegian who had come to Alaska looking for gold, travelled the first 400 of those kilometres. He had to trust his dog Togo's ability to find his way in the blinding snow and Togo turned out to be a reliable guide. The last part of the journey was done by Gunnar Kaasen who had driven dog teams in Alaska for 21 years. His lead dog was Balto. At one point Balto refused to go any further, and saved the team from falling into icy water. The diphtheria was stopped and Balto became a hero.

Nowadays a dog sled race is held every year from Anchorage to Nome, following the route of that famous journey in 1925. It is called the Iditarod and has become known as 'The Last Great Race on Earth'.

Part 4

Question 21–25

Read the text and questions below.
For each question, mark the correct letter **A**, **B**, **C** or **D** on your answer sheet.

Craigie Aitchison

The painter Craigie Aitchison was born in Scotland. He came to London intending to study law, but went to art school instead. There he found the traditional drawing classes difficult, but still kept on painting.

In his late twenties he was given money by the Italian government to study art, and became interested in early Italian artists, which shows in some of his work. He loved the greens and browns of the Italian fields and the clear light there, and wanted to put this light into his paintings.

This led him to paint colours thinly one on top of another from light to dark, but he insists he's never sure what the results will be. He says, 'It's a secret – because I don't know myself. I don't start by painting yellow, knowing I'm going to put anything on top.' Like most talented people, Aitchison makes it sound easy. 'Anyone can do the colours – you can buy them. I simply notice what you put the colours next to.'

Unlike some artists, he never does drawings before he starts a painting, as he feels that if he did, he might get bored and not do the painting afterwards. Instead, Aitchison changes his paintings many times before they are finished. This explains why his favourite models are people who don't ask to see their pictures while he's painting them. 'If I feel they're worried and want to look at the painting, I can't do it.'

Since moving to London years ago, he has not felt part of the Scottish painting scene. He says he is not interested in following any tradition, but just paints the way he can. However, his work still influences young British painters.

21   What is the writer trying to do in the text?

    A   describe particular works by Craigie Aitchison
    B   teach readers how to paint like Craigie Aitchison
    C   introduce readers to the artist Craigie Aitchison
    D   explain how Craigie Aitchison has made money from painting

22   What can the reader learn about Aitchison from the text?

    A   He works in a different way from other artists.
    B   He often gets bored with his paintings.
    C   He improved his drawing by going to art school.
    D   He did some paintings for the Italian government.

23 What does Aitchison say about his use of colour?

    A   He likes starting with the darkest colours first.

    B   He knows the colours he's aiming for when he begins.

    C   He prefers to paint with yellows, greens, and browns.

    D   He understands how different colours work together.

24 Aitchison prefers models who don't

    A   keep talking to him while he's working.

    B   ask him about his strange method of working.

    C   worry about how long the work will take.

    D   feel anxious to see the work as it's developing.

25 What might a visitor at an exhibition say about Aitchison's work?

A

> I love his recent paintings of Scotland, which are very similar to a number of other Scottish painters

B

> You can still see the influence of his trip to Italy in some of these pictures.

C

> You can tell he spent a lot of time drawing the picture before he started painting.

D

> I wonder if his law training helps him at all, especially in selling his work.

Part 5

Questions 26–35

Read the text below and choose the correct word for each space.
For each question, mark the correct letter **A**, **B**, **C** or **D** on your answer sheet.

Example:

| 0 | **A** keep | **B** stay | **C** hold | **D** rest |

Answer:

| 0 | **A** ▬ | **B** ▭ | **C** ▭ | **D** ▭ |

ZOOS

People began to **(0)** .... animals in zoos **(26)** .... 3,000 years ago, when the rulers of China opened an enormous zoo called the Gardens of Intelligence. In many of the early zoos, animals **(27)** .... taught to perform for the visitors. This no longer **(28)** .... and it is accepted that the purpose of zoos is for people to see animals behaving naturally.

Today, most cities have a zoo or wildlife park. However, not **(29)** .... approves of zoos. People who think that zoos are a good idea say they **(30)** .... us with the opportunity to **(31)** .... about the natural world and be close to wild animals. Both of **(32)** .... would not be possible **(33)** .... zoos. On the other hand, some people disapprove of zoos because they **(34)** .... it is wrong to put animals in cages, and argue that in zoos which are not **(35)** .... properly, animals live in dirty conditions and eat unsuitable food.

26	**A** above	**B** over	**C** more	**D** beyond
27	**A** are	**B** have	**C** were	**D** had
28	**A** appears	**B** becomes	**C** develops	**D** happens
29	**A** somebody	**B** everybody	**C** nobody	**D** anybody
30	**A** produce	**B** bring	**C** provide	**D** make
31	**A** discover	**B** learn	**C** find	**D** realise
32	**A** that	**B** what	**C** whose	**D** these
33	**A** without	**B** instead	**C** except	**D** unless
34	**A** hope	**B** expect	**C** imagine	**D** believe
35	**A** ordered	**B** managed	**C** decided	**D** aimed

WRITING

Part 1

Questions 1–5

Here are some sentences about a swimming pool.
For each question, complete the second sentence so that it means the same as the first.
Use no more than three words.
Write only the missing words on your answer sheet.
You may use this page for any rough work.

Example:

0   There is a new swimming pool in our town.

    Our town .... **a new swimming pool**.

Answer: | 0 | *has got* |

---

1   It's six months since I last went swimming.

    I .... **been swimming for six months**.

2   The new pool is near to my home.

    It's not .... **the new pool to my home**.

3   If you can't swim, you're not allowed in the deep end.

    You're not allowed in the deep end .... **you can swim**.

4   My friend Sam wanted me to go swimming with him.

    'Why .... **come swimming with me?' suggested Sam**.

5   I didn't go swimming with Sam because I was very busy.

    I was .... **busy to go swimming with Sam**.

Part 2

Question 6

A TV company came to your school yesterday to make a film.

Write an email to your English friend Alice. In your email, you should

- explain why the TV company chose your school
- tell her who or what they filmed
- say when the programme will be shown on television.

Write **35–45 words** on your answer sheet.

Part 3

Write an answer to **one** of the questions (**7** or **8**) in this part.
Write your answer in about **100 words** on your answer sheet.
Mark the question number in the box at the top of your answer sheet.

Question 7

- This is part of a letter you receive from an English friend.

> My parents want me to go on holiday with them this summer but I'd prefer to go somewhere with my friends. I have to choose. What do you think I should do?

- Now write a letter, giving your friend some advice.
- Write your **letter** on your answer sheet.

Question 8

- Your English teacher has asked you to write a story for homework.
- Your story must begin with this sentence:

As soon as I saw the handwriting on the envelope I smiled.

- Write your **story** on your answer sheet.

PAPER 2   LISTENING TEST

approx 35 minutes

(including 6 minutes transfer time)

Part 1

Questions 1–7

There are seven questions in this part.

For each question there are three pictures and a short recording.

Choose the correct picture and put a tick (✓) in the box below it.

Example: How many eggs do you need to make the cake?

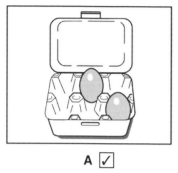 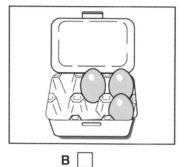 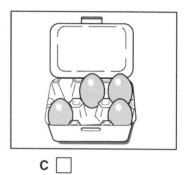

A ✓   B ☐   C ☐

---

1   Where are the dictionaries?

A ☐   B ☐   C ☐

2   Which evening dress does the woman decide to wear?

A ☐   B ☐   C ☐

3 What is the man's job now?

A ☐

B ☐

C ☐

4 Which calendar will the boy buy?

A ☐

B ☐

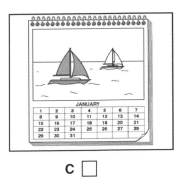

C ☐

5 What time will the writer arrive at the bookshop?

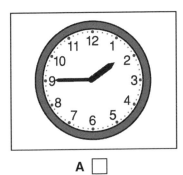

A ☐

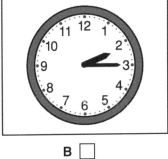

B ☐

C ☐

6 What did the woman leave in the restaurant?

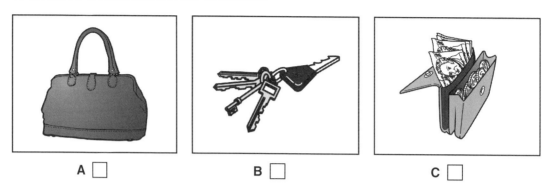

A ☐　　　　　B ☐　　　　　C ☐

7 Where is the bicycle?

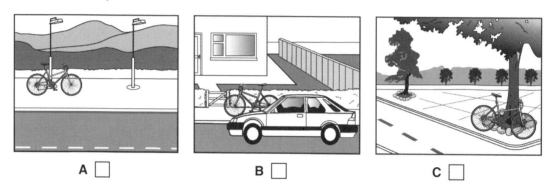

A ☐　　　　　B ☐　　　　　C ☐

Part 2

Questions 8–13

You will hear a radio interview with Jack Williams, who is talking about a town called Swanton. For each question, put a tick (✓) in the correct box.

8   Where is the town of Swanton located?

A ☐ near the sea

B ☐ by a lake

C ☐ on a hill

9   What does Jack like most about living in Swanton?

A ☐ There are opportunities for climbing nearby.

B ☐ There is plenty of activity in the town.

C ☐ There is interesting wildlife near the town.

10   What does Jack say about entertainment in Swanton?

A ☐ A music festival takes place in the town.

B ☐ Its football club has done well this year.

C ☐ An arts centre has recently opened.

11   Jack is worried about the environment of Swanton because

A ☐ the water in the river is dirty.

B ☐ there are few wild birds around today.

C ☐ pollution has destroyed the plants in one area.

12 What does Jack say about the way Swanton has changed?

A ☐ He preferred the town when it was smaller.

B ☐ He thinks it is a more interesting place.

C ☐ He is sorry that there are fewer jobs available.

13 Jack is positive about the future of Swanton because

A ☐ there is a successful new shopping centre.

B ☐ there will soon be a new airport.

C ☐ a new university is opening.

Part 3

Questions 14–19

You will hear a woman talking on the radio about a singing course she attended.
For each question, fill in the missing information in the numbered space.

Singing for Beginners

Place: Brownstoke College

Course details:

- Lena Phipps, a very good former **(14)** .... singer is the tutor

- the maximum number of students per course is **(15)** ....

- all classes start with exercises that help students to **(16)** ....

- students learn to sing **(17)** .... , modern and pop songs

- accommodation is in single or twin rooms

- cooked breakfast, lunch and dinner are included

- there's a very good lunch, especially **(18)** ....

Date the next course starts: **(19)** .... , 24th September

Part 4

Questions 20–25

Look at the six sentences for this part.

You will hear a conversation between a man, Marco, and his wife, Sarah, about a film they have just seen at the cinema.

Decide if each sentence is correct or incorrect.

If it is correct, put a tick (✓) in the box under **A** for **YES**. If it is not correct, put a tick (✓) in the box under **B** for **NO**.

		A YES	B NO
20	Sarah was expecting to enjoy the film.	☐	☐
21	Marco and Sarah agree that the city in the film was London.	☐	☐
22	Marco feels that the length of the film made it rather boring.	☐	☐
23	Sarah was upset about how some of the audience behaved during the film.	☐	☐
24	Sarah was disappointed with the way the main actor performed.	☐	☐
25	Marco thinks this film is the best the director has made.	☐	☐

About the Speaking test

The Speaking test lasts about 10 to 12 minutes. You take the test with another candidate. There are two examiners in the room. One examiner talks to you and the other examiner listens to you. Both the examiners give you marks.

Part 1

The examiners introduce themselves and then one examiner asks you and your partner to say your names and spell them. This examiner then asks you questions about yourself, your daily life, interests, etc.

Part 2

The examiner asks you to talk about something together and gives you a drawing to help you.

Part 3

You each have a chance to talk by yourselves. The examiner gives you a colour photograph to look at and asks you to talk about it. When you have finished talking, the examiner gives your partner a different photograph to look at and to talk about.

Part 4

The examiner asks you and your partner to say more about the subject of the photographs in Part 3. You may be asked to give your opinion or to talk about something that has happened to you.

Test 3

PAPER 1   READING AND WRITING TEST   (1 hour 30 minutes)

READING

Part 1

Questions 1–5

Look at the text in each question.
What does it say?
Mark the correct letter **A**, **B** or **C** on your answer sheet.

Example:

0

A Do not leave your bicycle touching the window.

B Broken glass may damage your bicycle tyres.

C Your bicycle may not be safe here.

Answer:

1

To   Elsa
From   Tony

Ranjit needs to know tomorrow whether we're going with him next month to his apartment in New York. Will your boss give you a week off?

Tony wants Elsa to

A ask her boss for a week's holiday starting tomorrow.

B find out if she can have time off next month.

C go away with him next week for a month.

2

CUSTOMERS

If the goods we have delivered are unsatisfactory, call us to arrange collection

A Ring and tell us if you are satisfied with the service we have delivered.

B Telephone us if arrangements for collecting goods are not satisfactory.

C Call us to take the goods back if you are not satisfied with them.

3

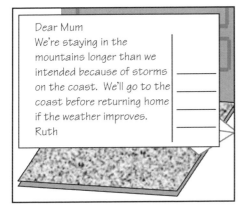

Dear Mum
We're staying in the mountains longer than we intended because of storms on the coast. We'll go to the coast before returning home if the weather improves.
Ruth

A Ruth has kept to her plan despite the change in the weather.

B Ruth may not visit the coast if the bad weather continues.

C Ruth intends to leave the mountains early to visit the coast.

4

The food in this container is not suitable for cooking in a microwave oven

A Remove this food from the container before placing in a microwave oven.

B It is advisable to use a suitable container for cooking this food.

C You should avoid putting this food in a microwave oven.

5

Library
Increased charges for borrowing DVDs will be in place from 1st January.

A You will have to pay more to borrow DVDs after 1st January.

B Please return all borrowed DVDs before 1st January.

C There will be additional DVDs to borrow from 1st January.

Part 2

Questions 6–10

The people below all want to hire somewhere for a party or event.
On the opposite page there are descriptions of eight places to hire.
Decide which place would be the most suitable for the following people.
For questions **6–10**, mark the correct letter (**A–H**) on your answer sheet.

6  Jessica is arranging her boss's retirement party. She is looking for somewhere in the town centre that can provide a traditional evening meal for around 100 guests.

7  Amelia is organising her 18th birthday party for 80 friends. She loves to dance and sing along to her favourite tunes. She wants to offer drinks and snacks rather than a sit-down meal.

8  James and Amanda need somewhere to hold their wedding party. They want to be able to take photos outdoors. Most of their 100 guests are coming by car and some will need overnight accommodation.

9  Jens wants to thank his staff of six by taking them out for a day in the countryside. He wants somewhere where they can do lots of fun activities and have a meal.

10  Sophie is organising her company's annual two-day conference. Several meeting rooms are required, one of which must be able to hold 200 people. They will all need to stay one night.

Places to Hire

A Rumbola

Rumbola is available for private bookings of up to 100 people. Hire one of our DJs, who will keep you and your guests moving to the music all night. If you know the words, he'll encourage you to join in! We have no restaurant, but light refreshments are available.

B The Darlington Centre

This modern building, situated in the countryside, is perfect for all business events. We have rooms of varying sizes – the Haversham is the largest with space for 300 people. Included in the price are meals, overnight accommodation and tea/coffee.

C Amazon Café

Situated in the town centre, this restaurant is an exciting place to celebrate a birthday or other special event. The restaurant is decorated to look and sound like a rainforest. Busy and fun, it is popular with young people who like Brazilian food and listening to loud music.

D Sunbury Park

This country house has space for 200 people at events such as weddings and formal dinners. In our beautiful park, we offer a variety of exciting sports and team-building games. As overnight accommodation is not provided, your event will be free from the interruptions often found in a hotel. We have a large car park.

E Narborough Manor

In the historic town centre, this beautiful hotel is the perfect setting for a wedding or birthday party. We can organise entertainment such as magic shows or live music. Lovely paintings and fireplaces make the perfect background for photos. Our dining room seats up to 80.

F Hudsons

This beautiful building dates from 1750 and is the last of its kind in this central location – all around it are shops and businesses. During the day it serves light lunches but in the evening it turns into an old-fashioned, formal restaurant, which can be hired for parties of up to 200 people.

G Hillcourt House

This family-run hotel is famous for its beautiful gardens. It can host private or small business events. The dining room holds 150 and meeting rooms hold 10-20. The hotel is in the countryside but close to two motorways and has plenty of parking spaces.

H Tiger Tom

At weekends, this stylish town-centre restaurant is full of famous faces, but on certain weekdays it can be hired for birthday parties or business events. The menus are modern and it is possible to play your own choice of music while you have your meal.

Part 3

Questions 11–20

Look at the sentences below about a hot-air balloon festival.
Read the text on the opposite page to decide if each sentence is correct or incorrect.
If it is correct, mark **A** on your answer sheet.
If it is not correct, mark **B** on your answer sheet.

---

11   The Albuquerque Balloon Festival lasts over a week.

12   The first festival took place at the opening of the local radio station.

13   The pilots use hand signals to communicate with each other.

14   The 'balloon glow' happens before sunrise and after sunset.

15   Members of the public are forbidden to enter the balloon take-off area.

16   Some advertising balloons join in the festival.

17   You can take a balloon ride to the top of the nearby mountains.

18   You can watch a firework show every evening of the festival.

19   The geography of the area around Albuquerque makes it particularly suitable for ballooning.

20   Visitors should be prepared for a range of temperatures.

The Albuquerque Balloon Festival

Every autumn, the sky above the desert city of Albuquerque in the south-western United States turns into a mass of bright colours. This is the Albuquerque Balloon Festival, an annual nine-day event.

The first festival was held in 1972 to celebrate the 50th birthday of the local radio station. There were about a dozen hot-air balloons and they took off from the car park in the middle of Albuquerque. From these small beginnings, the festival has grown steadily. This year at least a thousand balloons from over one third of the countries of the world are expected at its current out-of-town site.

What to see

The pilots are in radio contact with each other and all light up the burners of their balloons at the same time. These are known as 'balloon glows' and are an opportunity to take fantastic photographs. However, you must arrive just after night has fallen or before 5.30 am to see these 'glows' as the balloons rise into the dark sky.

During the day, you can walk around among the balloons and chat to the pilots as they prepare for take-off. The balloons come in all sizes and colours, some in the shapes of animals or cartoon characters – and, of course, well-known products such as varieties of soft drinks and fast food. Kids will love it.

In the afternoon, why not take to the sky yourself by arranging a balloon flight over the desert with one of the many companies offering balloon rides? Another possibility is to take the cable car from the desert floor to the top of the nearby mountains, the longest such ride anywhere, and enjoy a bird's-eye view of the festival. There are plenty of other attractions for visitors of all ages, including balloon races and firework displays on the opening evening and the last three evenings of the festival.

The Albuquerque Box

This is a local wind pattern that creates perfect conditions for balloonists. The Sandia Mountains protect the balloons from strong winds, and at the same time create gentler currents of wind at different heights. This means that by rising or descending, skilful pilots can control the direction of their balloons.

Practical advice

Buy your tickets in advance (they are available online) and save yourself a long wait to get into the festival site. Wear several layers of thin clothing. At night and in the early morning it can be quite cool, but during the day sunglasses and suncream are essential. Bring a flashlight for night-time events and, of course, bring your camera. If you're not a digital photographer, you'll need high-speed film for evening and night-time pictures.

Part 4

Questions 21–25

Read the text and questions below.
For each question, mark the correct letter **A**, **B**, **C** or **D** on your answer sheet.

The Young Achiever of the Year

Kal Kaur Rai has always been interested in fashion and has just won the title of *Young Achiever of the Year* at the Asian Business Awards. Ever since she was a child, she has drawn clothes and designed patterns. She never told her hard-working parents, who own a supermarket, that she wanted to turn her hobby into a career. She thought they expected her to go into a more established business, so she went to university to do a management degree.

After university, she moved to London and worked in an advertising agency. She had to attend industry events but couldn't afford the designer clothes she liked. She started making skirts and tops for herself. When her friends saw her clothes, they asked her to make things for them. She then found a small shop in London willing to take her designs on a sale-or-return basis. They were very popular and nothing came back. This encouraged her to leave her advertising job, take out a £20,000 loan and begin her own womenswear label.

Kal's parents were not angry about her career change and said they would support her, which really pleased her. Her clothes are now on sale in over 70 stores and her business has an income of over £500,000. Her clothes appear in fashion magazines, she designs for pop stars and she has just gained public recognition by winning this award. Her business has come a long way and she knows she is extremely lucky. 'What I do is my hobby – and I get paid for it! But remember, I've worked hard for this.'

21 What is the writer trying to do in the text?

    A   encourage fashion designers to make better business plans

    B   compare a job in fashion with other choices of career

    C   give details of recent changes in the fashion industry

    D   explain how a woman set up a fashion business

22 What does the reader learn about Kal's parents?

    A   They wanted Kal to help them run the family business.

    B   They did not realise that Kal wanted to work in fashion.

    C   They insisted Kal should continue with her job in advertising.

    D   They did not think Kal worked hard enough at university.

23   Kal decided to borrow £20,000 when

   A   all her clothes in the London shop were sold.
   B   her friends asked her to make clothes for them.
   C   she lost her job at the advertising agency.
   D   the fashion industry was in a period of growth.

24   What does Kal say about her career?

   A   She plans to open more stores.
   B   She believes that she deserves her success.
   C   She particularly enjoys designing for famous people.
   D   She expects more people to buy her clothes after the award.

25   What might Kal say now about her career?

   A   My management degree has helped me more than anything else. It's so important that young people interested in fashion can deal with money.

   B   I've learnt so much working for other fashion designers. Without this experience, I couldn't have started my own business.

   C   Running a fashion business is a dream come true and my parents being happy with my choice makes it even more special.

   D   Even when I was at university, my friends liked the clothes I made. This encouraged me to think about a career in fashion.

Part 5

Questions 26–35

Read the text below and choose the correct word for each space.
For each question, mark the correct letter **A**, **B**, **C** or **D** on your answer sheet.

Example:

| 0 | **A** in | **B** on | **C** at | **D** from |

Answer:

0	A B C D
	▬ ☐ ☐ ☐

Sweden's Ice Hotel

The village of Jukkasjärvi is **(0)** .... Swedish Lapland, and winter temperatures there can reach −40° C. But 6,000 holidaymakers **(26)** .... go there annually, to visit what is probably Europe's most unusual accommodation.

In this hotel you eat, drink, and sleep in rooms made **(27)** .... ice. If you want, you can **(28)** .... get married in one. The bar is ice too, and putting hot drinks on it is obviously not **(29)** .... ! The bedrooms are around −4° C, but fortunately guests are **(30)** .... with special sleeping bags that will keep **(31)** .... warm in the coldest of temperatures. **(32)** .... outdoor clothes can be supplied too, if needed.

The hotel is never more than six months old **(33)** .... it melts in summer, and **(34)** .... winter it is rebuilt. Creating the hotel **(35)** .... 10,000 tonnes of ice, plus 30,000 tonnes of snow.

26	**A** therefore	**B** ever	**C** also	**D** still
27	**A** by	**B** of	**C** within	**D** for
28	**A** even	**B** however	**C** already	**D** yet
29	**A** supported	**B** recognised	**C** recommended	**D** agreed
30	**A** given	**B** offered	**C** provided	**D** delivered
31	**A** these	**B** those	**C** they	**D** them
32	**A** Suitable	**B** Convenient	**C** Acceptable	**D** Satisfactory
33	**A** although	**B** because	**C** so	**D** while
34	**A** other	**B** any	**C** each	**D** another
35	**A** brings	**B** puts	**C** fetches	**D** takes

WRITING

PART 1

Questions 1–5

Here are some sentences about a well-known painting, *La Gioconda* (or *Mona Lisa*).
For each question, complete the second sentence so that it means the same as the first.
Use no more than three words.
Write only the missing words on your answer sheet.
You may use this page for any rough work.

Example:

0   It was 1503 when Leonardo da Vinci started to paint *La Gioconda*.

Leonardo da Vinci started to paint *La Gioconda* .... **1503**.

Answer: | **0** | *in* |

---

1   Probably, no other painting is as famous as *La Gioconda*.

La Gioconda is probably .... **painting in the world**.

2   Nobody is sure of the identity of the woman in the painting.

Nobody is sure .... **the woman in the painting is**.

3   People find the smile of the woman in the painting interesting.

People are .... **in the smile of the woman in the painting**.

4   It took Leonardo a long time to paint this picture.

Leonardo spent a long time .... **this picture**.

5   Does anyone know what this picture is worth today?

Does anyone know how .... **this picture is worth today?**

Part 2

Question 6

You arranged to meet your English friend Sally next Tuesday, but you have to change the time.

Write an email to Sally. In your email, you should

- suggest a new time to meet on Tuesday
- explain why you need to change the time
- remind Sally where you arranged to meet.

Write **35–45 words** on your answer sheet.

Part 3

Write an answer to **one** of the questions (**7** or **8**) in this part.
Write your answer in about **100 words** on your answer sheet.
Mark the question number in the box at the top of your answer sheet.

Question 7

- Your Scottish penfriend has written to you for advice.

Next month, I'm moving with my family to a different area. I have
to choose between going to a small school in the countryside or
a large school in the centre of town. What should I do?

- Now write a letter to your penfriend, giving your advice.
- Write your **letter** on your answer sheet.

Question 8

- Your English teacher has asked you to write a story.
- Your story must begin with this sentence:

As the man left the café, Maria saw that his phone was still on the table.

- Write your **story** on your answer sheet.

PAPER 2 LISTENING TEST approx 35 minutes
(including 6 minutes transfer time)

Part 1

Questions 1–7

There are seven questions in this part.
For each question there are three pictures and a short recording.
Choose the correct picture and put a tick (✓) in the box below it.

Example: How did the woman get to work?

  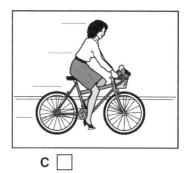

A ✓   B ☐   C ☐

---

1   What regular exercise does David do at the moment?

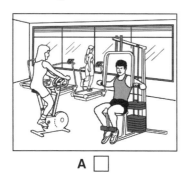 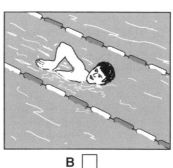 

A ☐   B ☐   C ☐

2   What should Suzie take to Emma's house?

 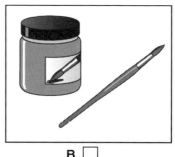 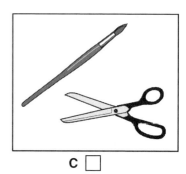

A ☐   B ☐   C ☐

3   Which kind of T-shirt did the boy choose?

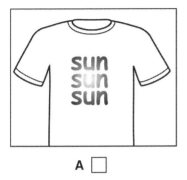   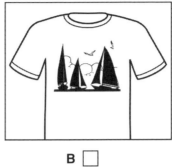   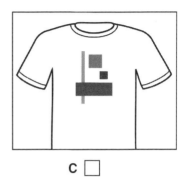

A ☐   B ☐   C ☐

4   What frightened the man?

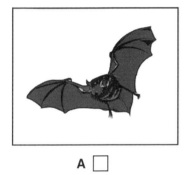      

A ☐   B ☐   C ☐

5   Where is the man calling from?

A ☐   B ☐   C ☐

6   How did the woman spend her last holiday?

A ☐   B ☐   C ☐

7   Where is the girl's purse?

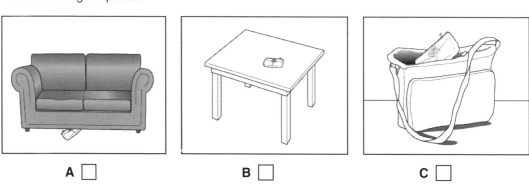

A ☐   B ☐   C ☐

Part 2

Questions 8–13

You will hear a radio interview with a ballet dancer called Elena Karpov, who is talking about her life and career.

For each question, put a tick (✓) in the correct box.

---

8   Elena decided to become a dancer when she was

A ☐ seven.

B ☐ nine.

C ☐ eleven.

9   At ballet school in New York, Elena

A ☐ was the only student from Bulgaria.

B ☐ found learning the language hard.

C ☐ learned to be independent.

10   What does Elena say about the ballet called *Cinderella*?

A ☐ Children will enjoy it.

B ☐ The music was unfamiliar to her.

C ☐ She saw it when she was a child.

11   In her free time, Elena likes to

A ☐ go sightseeing.

B ☐ go to clubs.

C ☐ go shopping.

12   What does Elena often do for her fans?

    A ☐ She gives them a flower.

    B ☐ She signs one of her photographs.

    C ☐ She sends them a free ticket.

13   What does Elena like best about her job?

    A ☐ appearing on television

    B ☐ doing something she loves

    C ☐ travelling to different countries

Part 3

Questions 14–19

You will hear a group leader talking to some students who are going to visit an important athletics event in Birmingham.

For each question, fill in the missing information in the numbered space.

Athletics Championships

Date of college trip: **(14)** 15th ....

Number of sportspeople who will compete: **(15)** ....

How the group will travel to Birmingham: by **(16)** ....

What group members should take on the day: **(17)** ....

Name of the website page: **(18)** ....

Which day other details will be available to students: **(19)** ....

Part 4

Questions 20–25

Look at the six sentences for this part.
You will hear two friends, a boy, Rolf, and a girl, Maria, talking about the jobs they would like to do in the future.
Decide if each sentence is correct or incorrect.
If it is correct, put a tick (✓) in the box under **A** for **YES**. If it is not correct, put a tick (✓) in the box under **B** for **NO**.

		A YES	B NO
20	Maria would like to travel a lot as part of her job.	☐	☐
21	Maria is confident she will be able to work for an airline.	☐	☐
22	Rolf intends to do a job connected with his degree.	☐	☐
23	Maria and Rolf agree it is important to have a good salary.	☐	☐
24	Maria hopes to work for several different employers.	☐	☐
25	Rolf's ambition is to manage his own company one day.	☐	☐

About the Speaking test

The Speaking test lasts about 10 to 12 minutes. You take the test with another candidate. There are two examiners in the room. One examiner talks to you and the other examiner listens to you. Both the examiners give you marks.

Part 1

The examiners introduce themselves and then one examiner asks you and your partner to say your names and spell them. This examiner then asks you questions about yourself, your daily life, interests, etc.

Part 2

The examiner asks you to talk about something together and gives you a drawing to help you.

Part 3

You each have a chance to talk by yourselves. The examiner gives you a colour photograph to look at and asks you to talk about it. When you have finished talking, the examiner gives your partner a different photograph to look at and to talk about.

Part 4

The examiner asks you and your partner to say more about the subject of the photographs in Part 3. You may be asked to give your opinion or to talk about something that has happened to you.

Test 4

PAPER 1   READING AND WRITING TEST   (1 hour 30 minutes)

READING

Part 1

Questions 1–5

Look at the text in each question.
What does it say?
Mark the correct letter **A**, **B** or **C** on your answer sheet.

Example:

0

A Valuable objects are removed at night.

B Valuables should not be left in the van.

C This van is locked at night.

Answer:

1

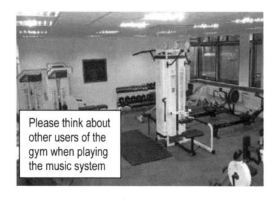

A The members of the gym think the music system is very useful.

B When using the music system in the gym, please remember to switch it off.

C If you put on some music, consider the other people in the gym.

2

> Having a great time.
> Some of the group
> have returned home,
> but the rest of us are
> having a boat trip
> tomorrow.
> See you next week.

The writer is

A going home with the rest of the group tomorrow.

B going on a boat with members of the group tomorrow.

C going out with the whole group tomorrow.

3

> **English Library**
>
> All books are arranged
> in A-Z order.
> Please put them back
> correctly

A You should return your books to the assistant in the correct order.

B The books are easy to find because they are all arranged by level.

C You should replace books in the order that you found them.

4

> *If entrance
> door is locked,
> please press
> button to
> contact hotel
> reception.*

A Use this button to call hotel staff if you cannot get in.

B If you cannot lock the door, please contact hotel reception.

C Press this button to unlock the entrance door.

5

> David
> I'll be back late. Don't
> forget Carla needs a lift
> to band practice at
> school – please make
> sure she's in uniform.
>   Marta

What should David do?

A He should remind Carla that someone is picking her up for band practice.

B He should check Carla is dressed properly and take her to band practice.

C He should make Carla practise before she goes to her school band meeting.

Part 2

Questions 6–10

The people below are all on holiday in the north of England and want to go for a walk in the countryside.
On the opposite page there are descriptions of eight country walks.
Decide which walk would be the most suitable for the following people.
For questions **6–10** mark the correct letter (**A–H**) on your answer sheet.

---

6  Mary and George, a retired couple, want to go on a short walk that lasts about an hour. They like old houses and pretty countryside, but can't climb steep hills.

7  The Thompson family want to spend a day out, including lunch. The parents like visiting gardens, but aren't interested in country houses. The two children are very active and like animals.

8  Carolina and Juan are experienced, independent walkers. They would like a long walk followed by a meal in a pub. Although they like attractive old villages, they don't enjoy crowded places.

9  Kenzo would like to join an organised walk to learn about the area. He is interested in history and wants to see one of the best-known places in this part of the country.

10  Belinda and her young teenage son Tom both enjoy being outdoors. Belinda wants to go walking and then find a nice café to relax in. Tom gets bored just walking and prefers other activities, especially sports.

Country Walks

A Lime House and Country Park

The house attracts thousands of visitors, but this is a pleasant walk (for the fit!) away from the crowds, through parkland, woods and up onto the hills. Popular with bird-watchers. Allow three hours. The house was built in 1570. Gardens closed to the public; information centre, café and souvenir shop open daily.

B Howden Lake

This two-hour walk attracts thousands of visitors. When the water is low, you can see a village which was flooded 300 years ago. Quiet café with beautiful views. Children can go sailing and windsurfing on the lake with trained instructors.

C Devonshire Park

Take a really enjoyable walk in the countryside surrounding the park. Allow at least half a day, or make it a full day by visiting the adventure playground and farmyard (both great for young children). Stop at the café (open all day) or enjoy the fantastic gardens, with beautiful fountains. Guided walks available for small groups.

D Stanton

This walk is definitely for very fit walkers only – the tracks get very slippery after rain. Allow six hours and start early! You're unlikely to meet another person all day. Fantastic views of farmland in the valleys below. Be sure to pack sandwiches – you'll be up on the hilltops all day.

E Hope Village

A leisurely way to spend an hour or two is by visiting the busy village of Hope with its lovely old cottages, traditional pubs and country gardens. A gentle walk towards the hills will soon bring you to superb views.

F Strines

You need to be used to walking to successfully complete this seven-hour walk through the wildest scenery in the area. Follow a little-known footpath to the highest point for miles. The traditional pub down in the village serves hot food from 12.00 daily.

G Cornford

This is an easy walk through a little-known valley beside clear streams with woodland flowers, birds and animals. See the 200-year-old buildings from the cloth-making industry which now stand empty. Private tours can be arranged. Allow half a day for the walk.

H Langsett

After a steep climb, this is an exciting walk along easy paths, which are crowded at weekends (people come from all over Britain to climb Langsett). The views are dramatic, and it's a popular place for family picnics. Guided walks start from the nearby village (10 am Sundays) and visit 800-year-old woodland and ruins dating back two thousand years.

Part 3

Questions 11–20

Look at the sentences below about a competition.
Read the text on the opposite page to decide if each sentence is correct or incorrect.
If it is correct, mark **A** on your answer sheet.
If it is not correct, mark **B** on your answer sheet.

---

11 All prize winners will have their stories printed in the magazine *Keep Writing*.

12 Most people entering the competition last year followed the advice they were given.

13 Writers should remember to check that any information they use is correct.

14 The magazine is looking for stories which have an unexpected ending.

15 Writers are encouraged to describe the people in their stories clearly.

16 Stories should either be written clearly by hand or typed.

17 Late entries can be faxed if necessary.

18 The magazine will send back all stories which have failed to be selected.

19 The rules of the competition are different this year from last year.

20 Writers can enter stories which magazines outside Britain have already printed.

Write a winning story!

You could win £1,000 in this year's Fiction Prize and have your story printed in Keep Writing magazine. Ten other lucky people will win a cheque for £100.

Once again, we need people who can write good stories. The judges, who include Mary Littlejohn, the novelist, Michael Brown, the television reporter, and Susan Hitchins, *Keep Writing's* editor, are looking for interesting and original stories. Detective fiction was extremely popular last year, although the competition winner produced a love story. You can write about whatever you want but here's some advice to start you thinking:

- **Write about what you know**

This is the advice which every writer should pay attention to and, last year, nearly everyone who wrote for us did exactly that. Love, family, problems with friends – these were the main subjects of the stories. However, you need to turn ordinary situations into something interesting that people will want to read about. Make the reader want to continue reading by writing about ordinary things in a new and surprising way.

- **Get your facts right**

It's no good giving a description of a town or explaining how a jet engine works if you get it wrong. So avoid writing anything unless you're certain about it.

- **Hold the reader's attention**

Make the beginning interesting and the ending a surprise. There is nothing worse than a poor ending. Develop the story carefully and try to think of something unusual happening at the end.

- **Think about the characters**

Try to bring the people in your story alive for the reader by using well-chosen words to make them seem real.

Your story must be your own work, between 2,000 and 2,500 words and typed, double-spaced, on one side only of each sheet of paper.

Even if you're in danger of missing the closing date, we are unable to accept stories by fax or email. You must include the application form with your story. Unfortunately your story cannot be returned, nor can we discuss our decisions.

You should not have had any fiction printed in any magazine or book in this country – a change in the rules by popular request – and the story must not have appeared in print or in recorded form, for example on radio or TV, anywhere in the world.

Your fee of £5 will go to the Writers' Association. Make your cheque payable to *Keep Writing* and send it with the application form and your story to:

Keep Writing
75 Broad Street
Birmingham
B12 4TG

The closing date is 30 July and we will inform the winner within one month of this date. Please note that if you win, you must agree to have your story printed in our magazine.

Part 4

Questions 21–25

Read the text and questions below.
For each question, mark the correct letter **A**, **B**, **C** or **D** on your answer sheet.

Being an older student

At 32, I have just finished my first year at university. As well as attending lectures regularly, I have had to learn to read books quickly and write long essays.

I decided to go to university after fourteen years away from the classroom. As a secretary, although I was earning a reasonable amount of money, I was bored doing something where I hardly had to think. I became more and more depressed by the idea that I was stuck in the job. I was jealous of the students at the local university, who looked happy, carefree and full of hope, and part of something that I wanted to explore further.

However, now that I've actually become a student I find it hard to mix with younger colleagues. They are always mistaking me for a lecturer and asking me questions I can't answer. I also feel separated from the lecturers because, although we are the same age, I know so much less than them. But I am glad of this opportunity to study because I know you need a qualification to get a rewarding job, which is really important to me. Unlike most eighteen-year-olds, I much prefer a weekend with my books to one out partying. Then there are the normal student benefits of long holidays and theatre and cinema discounts. I often have doubts about what I'll do after university, but I hope that continuing my education at this late date has been a wise choice.

---

21 What is the writer trying to do in the text?

    A   help lecturers understand older students
    B   explain her reasons for returning to study
    C   suggest some good methods for studying
    D   complain about the attitude of young students

22 What can a reader find out about the writer from this text?

    A   when she left school
    B   how long her university course is
    C   where she will work in future
    D   what subject she is studying

23 How did the writer feel about her job as a secretary?

   A Her salary wasn't good enough.
   B It gave her the opportunity to study.
   C It didn't make use of her brain.
   D Her colleagues made her depressed.

24 In her spare time, the writer likes to

   A go out to parties.
   B earn some money.
   C travel a lot.
   D do extra study.

25 Which of these sentences describes the writer?

A She realises the value of a university degree.

B She gets on well with the other students.

C She is confident about the future.

D She finds university life easier than she expected.

Part 5

Questions 26–35

Read the text below and choose the correct word for each space.
For each question, mark the correct letter **A**, **B**, **C** or **D** on your answer sheet.

Example:

| 0 | **A** on | **B** of | **C** to | **D** out |

Answer:

0	A B C D
	■ □ □ □

Henry Ford

Henry Ford was born **(0)** .... a farm in Michigan in 1863 but he did not like farming. When he was fifteen he began work as a mechanic and in 1893 he built his first car. After he **(26)** .... driven it 1,500 kilometres, he sold it and built two bigger cars. Then, in 1903, he **(27)** .... the Ford Motor Company. By **(28)** .... strong but light steel, he built cheap cars for **(29)** .... people to buy. In 1908, he built the first Ford Model 'T', **(30)** .... sold for $825. He was soon selling 100 cars **(31)** .... day. By 1927, the Ford Motor Company was **(32)** .... $700 million. Early Ford cars were simple and cheap, but **(33)** .... things simple sometimes **(34)** .... less choice. 'You **(35)** .... have any colour you like,' said Henry Ford of the Model T, 'as long as it's black.'

26	**A** is	**B** was	**C** had	**D** has
27	**A** raised	**B** started	**C** led	**D** appeared
28	**A** putting	**B** operating	**C** using	**D** managing
29	**A** usual	**B** ordinary	**C** general	**D** typical
30	**A** where	**B** which	**C** who	**D** what
31	**A** a	**B** some	**C** the	**D** one
32	**A** rich	**B** worth	**C** expensive	**D** dear
33	**A** remaining	**B** staying	**C** keeping	**D** holding
34	**A** meant	**B** decided	**C** planned	**D** intended
35	**A** will	**B** ought	**C** need	**D** can

Visual material for the Speaking test

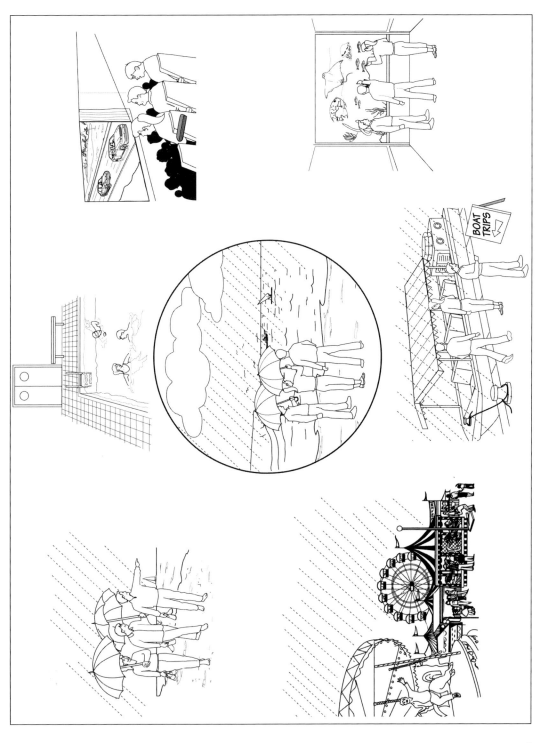

1B

2C

2A

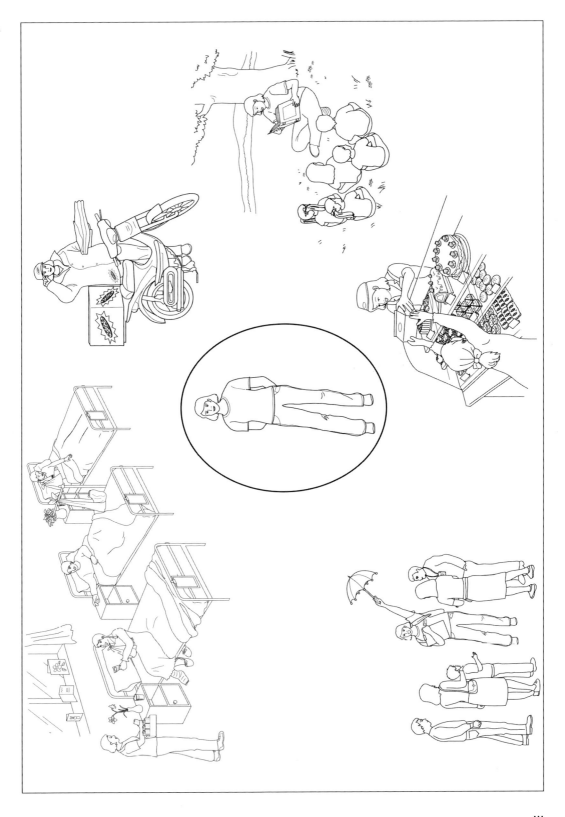

2B

1C

3A

3B

4C

4A

4B

3C

WRITING

Part 1

Questions 1–5

Here are some sentences about a school trip to a museum.
For each question, complete the second sentence so that it means the same as the first.
Use no more than three words.
Write only the missing words on your answer sheet.
You may use this page for any rough work.

Example:

0   Mr Winters told the class they were going to visit the museum.

  Mr Winters said to the class, '.. to visit the museum.'

Answer: | **0** | *We're going* |

---

1   The museum was near the school.

  The museum was not .... the school.

2   It cost £3 to visit the museum.

  They had to .... £3 to visit the museum.

3   The class was taken around the museum by a guide.

  A museum guide .... around the museum.

4   They did not leave until 4 o'clock.

  It was 4 o'clock .... they left the museum.

5   Everybody thought that the museum visit was boring.

  Everybody was .... by the museum visit.

Part 2

Question 6

Your friend Alex has invited you to go to the cinema tomorrow, but you can't go.

Write an email to Alex. In your email, you should

- apologise
- explain why you can't go
- invite Alex to do something with you another day.

Write **35–45 words** on your answer sheet.

Part 3

Write an answer to **one** of the questions (**7** or **8**) in this part.
Write your answer in about **100 words** on your answer sheet.
Mark the question number in the box at the top of your answer sheet.

Question 7

- This is part of a letter you receive from an English friend.

> We had dinner at a new restaurant yesterday. It was great! How often do you eat out? What's your favourite restaurant like?

- Now write a letter, answering your friend's questions.
- Write your **letter** on your answer sheet.

Question 8

- Your English teacher has asked you to write a story.
- Your story must begin with this sentence:

I had a real surprise when I turned on the television.

- Write your **story** on your answer sheet.

PAPER 2   LISTENING TEST   approx 35 minutes
(including 6 minutes transfer time)

Part 1

Questions 1–7

There are seven questions in this part.
For each question there are three pictures and a short recording.
Choose the correct picture and put a tick (✓) in the box below it.

Example: How did the woman get to work?

A ✓   B ☐   C ☐

---

1   What did the thieves steal?

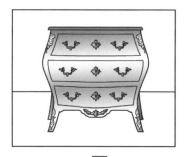   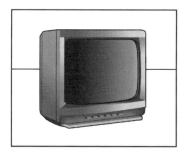

A ☐   B ☐   C ☐

2   What present will they take?

A ☐   B ☐   C ☐

3 What will the woman eat tonight?

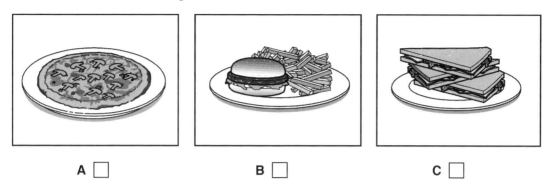

A ☐   **B** ☐   **C** ☐

4 How much will the girl's ticket cost?

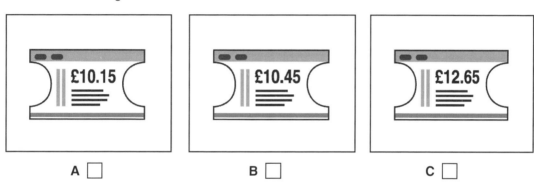

A ☐   **B** ☐   **C** ☐

5 What is the grandmother's job now?

A ☐   **B** ☐   **C** ☐

6   Which button has the boy lost?

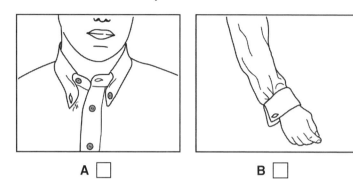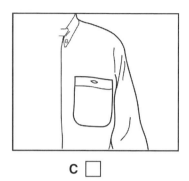

A ☐   B ☐   C ☐

7   What will the man do first?

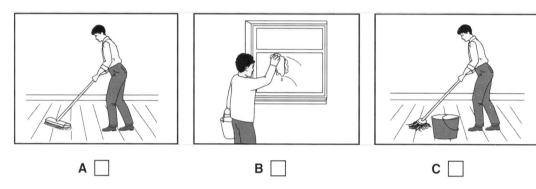

A ☐   B ☐   C ☐

Part 2

Questions 8–13

You will hear Sarah Brown talking about her work as a television weather forecaster.
For each question put a tick (✓) in the correct box.

---

8 How long has Sarah worked as a weather forecaster?

    A ☐ two years

    B ☐ seven years

    C ☐ thirty years

9 What does Sarah say about her job?

    A ☐ She sometimes has to work at night.

    B ☐ She enjoys getting up early.

    C ☐ She works ten or twelve hours a day.

10 When Sarah does a weather forecast,

    A ☐ she prepares it in advance.

    B ☐ she sometimes forgets her words.

    C ☐ she worries about making a mistake.

11 Sarah's husband

    A ☐ works on the same days each week.

    B ☐ wants to move nearer his work.

    C ☐ spends a lot of time travelling.

12 Sarah is pleased because she

A ☐ has got her pilot's licence.

B ☐ taught her husband to play tennis.

C ☐ took part in a long race.

13 A man in India wanted

A ☐ to meet Sarah's family.

B ☐ a photo of Sarah.

C ☐ to receive a letter from Sarah.

Part 3

Questions 14–19

You will hear a radio talk about holidays in Northumberland.
For each question fill in the missing information in the numbered space.

Holidays in Northumberland

Useful Information

- Read Peter Green's book called '**(14)** .... *around Northumberland*'.
- Lots of things to see, for example **(15)** ....
- Accommodation in flats, hotels, cottages or bed and breakfast places.
- Best time to go is **(16)** ....

Bike Hire

- One week – £35
- Two weeks – **(17)** £ ....

Local Events

- June – *Food Festival*
- August – *International Festival of* **(18)** ....

National Park Activities

- Guided walks
- Photography
- **(19)** ....

Part 4

Questions 20–25

Look at the six sentences for this part.
You will hear a conversation between a girl called Julia and her father, about choosing a course at university.
Decide if each sentence is correct or incorrect.
If it is correct, put a tick (✓) in the box under **A** for **YES**. If it is not correct, put a tick (✓) in the box under **B** for **NO**.

		A YES	B NO
20	Julia wants to choose a course as soon as possible.	☐	☐
21	Julia's father thinks that studying business may be boring.	☐	☐
22	Julia's father believes Julia's friend is making the wrong choice.	☐	☐
23	Julia's father thinks she might find studying business too difficult.	☐	☐
24	Julia is confident about her maths.	☐	☐
25	Julia is keen to consider her father's suggestion.	☐	☐

About the Speaking test

The Speaking test lasts about 10 to 12 minutes. You take the test with another candidate. There are two examiners in the room. One examiner talks to you and the other examiner listens to you. Both the examiners give you marks.

Part 1

The examiners introduce themselves and then one examiner asks you and your partner to say your names and spell them. This examiner then asks you questions about yourself, your daily life, interests, etc.

Part 2

The examiner asks you to talk about something together and gives you a drawing to help you.

Part 3

You each have a chance to talk by yourselves. The examiner gives you a colour photograph to look at and asks you to talk about it. When you have finished talking, the examiner gives your partner a different photograph to look at and to talk about.

Part 4

The examiner asks you and your partner to say more about the subject of the photographs in Part 3. You may be asked to give your opinion or to talk about something that has happened to you.

UNIVERSITY *of* **CAMBRIDGE**
ESOL Examinations

S A M P L E

Candidate Name
If not already printed, write name
in CAPITALS and complete the
Candidate No. grid (in pencil).

Candidate Signature

Examination Title

Centre

Supervisor:
If the candidate is ABSENT or has WITHDRAWN shade here ▭

Centre No.

Candidate No.

Examination
Details

0	0	0	0
1	1	1	1
2	2	2	2
3	3	3	3
4	4	4	4
5	5	5	5
6	6	6	6
7	7	7	7
8	8	8	8
9	9	9	9

PET Paper 1 Reading and Writing Candidate Answer Sheet 1

Instructions

Use a PENCIL (B or HB).

Rub out any answer you want to change with an eraser.

For **Reading:**
Mark ONE letter for each question.
For example, if you think **A** is the right answer to the
question, mark your answer sheet like this:

Part 1

1	A B C
2	A B C
3	A B C
4	A B C
5	A B C

Part 2

6	A B C D E F G H
7	A B C D E F G H
8	A B C D E F G H
9	A B C D E F G H
10	A B C D E F G H

Part 3

11	A B
12	A B
13	A B
14	A B
15	A B
16	A B
17	A B
18	A B
19	A B
20	A B

Part 4

21	A B C D
22	A B C D
23	A B C D
24	A B C D
25	A B C D

Part 5

26	A B C D
27	A B C D
28	A B C D
29	A B C D
30	A B C D
31	A B C D
32	A B C D
33	A B C D
34	A B C D
35	A B C D

Continue on the other side of this sheet ⟶

PET RW 1

DP491/389

S A M P L E

For **Writing (Parts 1 and 2):**

Write your answers clearly in the spaces provided.

Part 1: Write your answers below.	Do not write here
1	1 1 0
2	1 2 0
3	1 3 0
4	1 4 0
5	1 5 0

Part 2 (Question 6): Write your answer below.

Put your answer to Writing Part 3 on Answer Sheet 2 ➡

Do not write below (Examiner use only)					
0	1	2	3	4	5

UNIVERSITY of CAMBRIDGE
ESOL Examinations

S A M P L E

PET Paper 1 Reading and Writing   Candidate Answer Sheet 2

Candidate Instructions:

Write your answer to Writing Part 3
on the other side of this sheet.

Use a PENCIL (B or HB).

This section for use by FIRST Examiner only

Mark:

0	1.1	1.2	1.3	2.1	2.2	2.3	3.1	3.2	3.3	4.1	4.2	4.3	5.1	5.2	5.3

Examiner Number:

	0 1 2 3 4 5 6 7 8 9
	0 1 2 3 4 5 6 7 8 9
	0 1 2 3 4 5 6 7 8 9
	0 1 2 3 4 5 6 7 8 9

94

S A M P L E

Do not write below this line

This section for use by SECOND Examiner only

Mark:

0	1.1	1.2	1.3	2.1	2.2	2.3	3.1	3.2	3.3	4.1	4.2	4.3	5.1	5.2	5.3

Examiner Number:

	0 1 2 3 4 5 6 7 8 9
	0 1 2 3 4 5 6 7 8 9
	0 1 2 3 4 5 6 7 8 9
	0 1 2 3 4 5 6 7 8 9

Sample answer sheet: Paper 2

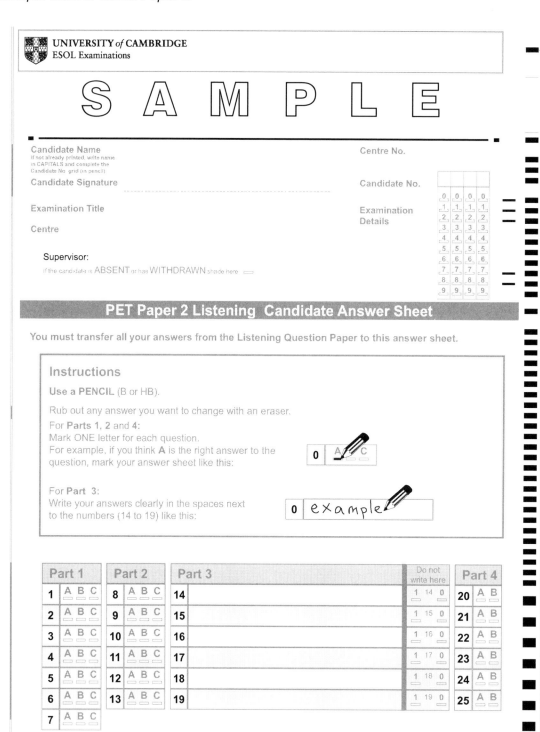

Acknowledgements

The authors and publishers acknowledge the following sources of copyright material and are grateful for the permissions granted. While every effort has been made, it has not always been possible to identify the sources of all the material used, or to trace all copyright holders. If any omissions are brought to our notice, we will be happy to include the appropriate acknowledgements on reprinting.

Royal Academy of Arts for the adapted text on p. 38 'Craigie Aitchison' by Laura Gascoigne. First published in *RA Magazine* number 80, Autumn 2003, the magazine of the Royal Academy of Arts. Reproduced by permission.

Colour section

Alamy for p. II(2C)/Simon Barber; Getty Images for p. VI(3B)/ Shuji Kobayashi; Masterfile for pp. IV(1C)/Andrew Olney, VI(4C)/David Mendelsohn, VIII(3C)/Paul Wright; Stockbroker for pp. II(1C)/Goodshoot, VIII(4B)/Martin Ley.

Black and white section

Alamy for pp. 74(10)/Blue Moon Stock; Asian Woman magazine www.asianwomanmag.com for p. 58; Corbis for p. 57/Vince Streano; Getty Images for p. 14(7) and p. 34(10)/Nisian Hughes, p. 34(6)/Jetta Productions, p. 34(7)/Harald Eisenberger, p. 54(8)/Yellow Dog Productions, p. 60/Arctic-Images, p. 74(9)/Ariel Skelley; PA Photos for p. 20/Patrick Seeger/DPA; Photofusion Picture Library for p. 74(8)/Ute Klaphake; Photolibrary.com for p. 14(6 & 8)/Monkey Business Images Ltd, p. 14(10)/Michael Turek, p. 34(9)/Stockbroker, p. 54(6)/Rudolf Reiner, p. 54(7)/Richard Ross, p. 54(9)/Jeremy Maude, p. 54(10)/Paul Thomas, p. 74(7)/ Bananastock, Punchstock for p. 34(8)/imagenavi; Shutterstock for pp. 14(9), 74(6).

Picture research by Kevin Brown.

Design concept by Peter Ducker MSTD

The CDs which accompany this book were recorded at dsound, London